Brazil

by Colleen Sexton

ORDEM E PROGRESSO

BELLWETHER MEDIA • MINNEAPOLIS, MN

Note to Librarians, Teachers, and Parents:

Blastoff! Readers are carefully developed by literacy experts and combine standards-based content with developmentally appropriate text.

Level 1 provides the most support through repetition of high-frequency words, light text, predictable sentence patterns, and strong visual support.

Level 2 offers early readers a bit more challenge through varied simple sentences, increased text load, and less repetition of high-frequency words.

Level 3 advances early-fluent readers toward fluency through increased text and concept load, less reliance on visuals, longer sentences, and more literary language.

Level 4 builds reading stamina by providing more text per page, increased use of punctuation, greater variation in sentence patterns, and increasingly challenging vocabulary.

Level 5 encourages children to move from "learning to read" to "reading to learn" by providing even more text, varied writing styles, and less familiar topics.

Whichever book is right for your reader, Blastoff! Readers are the perfect books to build confidence and encourage a love of reading that will last a lifetime!

This edition first published in 2011 by Bellwether Media, Inc.

No part of this publication may be reproduced in whole or in part without written permission of the publisher. For information regarding permission, write to Bellwether Media, Inc., Attention: Permissions Department, 5357 Penn Avenue South, Minneapolis, MN 55419.

Library of Congress Cataloging-in-Publication Data

Sexton, Colleen A., 1967-
Brazil / by Colleen Sexton.
   p. cm. – (Exploring countries) (Blastoff! Readers)
Includes bibliographical references and index.
Summary: "Developed by literacy experts for students in grades three through seven, this book introduces young readers to the geography and culture of Brazil"–Provided by publisher.
ISBN 978-1-60014-474-5 (hardcover : alk. paper)
 1. Brazil–Juvenile literature. I. Title.
F2508.5.S47 2010
981–dc22   2010018730

Printed in the United States of America, North Mankato, MN.

080110   1162

Contents

Where Is Brazil?   4

The Land   6

The Amazon Rain Forest   8

Wildlife   10

The People   12

Daily Life   14

Going to School   16

Working   18

Playing   20

Food   22

Holidays   24

Christ the Redeemer   26

Fast Facts   28

Glossary   30

To Learn More   31

Index   32

Guyana

Venezuela

Suriname

Colombia

French Guiana

Ecuador

Brazil

Peru

Brasília
★

Bolivia

Rio de Janeiro

Chile

Paraguay

São Paulo

**Pacific
Ocean**

Argentina

Uruguay

Did you know?
About 19 million people live
in and around São Paulo.
It is Brazil's largest city and the
seventh-largest city in the world.

Brazil is the largest country in South America. With an area of 3,287,612 square miles (8,514,877 square kilometers), it covers almost half the **continent**! Brazil is diamond shaped. The western half borders ten other South American countries. Only Ecuador and Chile do not touch Brazil.

The eastern half of Brazil extends into the Atlantic Ocean to create a coastline that is more than 4,600 miles (7,400 kilometers) long. Most of Brazil's large cities lie on or near the coast. They include Rio de Janeiro and São Paulo. Brasília is Brazil's capital. It lies about 600 miles (965 kilometers) inland from the coast.

Atlantic Ocean

Brazil is known for the variety and beauty of its landscapes. Sandy beaches and rocky shores line the coast. In the far north, the Guiana Highlands rise into the clouds. South of these mountain peaks, the thick Amazon Rain Forest covers northwestern Brazil. A dry plain called the *sertão* lies in the northeast.

A high, grassy **plateau** stretches across the middle of the country. It surrounds the mountain peaks of the Serra Geral and meets the rest of the Serra do Mar in the southeast. The south features rich, red soil that is good for farming. Broad plains called *pampas* cover the far south. There, cowboys, or *gaúchos*, herd cattle on huge ranches.

fun fact

Iguaçu Falls, found on Brazil's southwestern border, is about 2 miles (3.2 kilometers) wide. Its waters tumble down as far as 269 feet (82 meters). The thundering roar of Iguaçu Falls can be heard from miles away!

Iguaçu Falls

fun fact

The Amazon River carries more water than any other river on Earth. More than 1,000 rivers and streams flow into it. In many places, the Amazon River is several miles wide!

The Amazon Rain Forest is the world's largest **tropical rain forest**. Most of this thick jungle lies in Brazil, where it is called *Amazônia*. It gets its name from the mighty Amazon River, which winds eastward through the rain forest and empties into the Atlantic Ocean. Many **native** peoples live in the Amazon, and have for hundreds of years.

Did you know?
The Amazon Rain Forest is in danger. Loggers cut down trees to make wood products. Farmers clear the land to grow crops and raise livestock. Many groups are working to save the rain forest and the animals and people that live there.

A rain forest grows in layers. The tops of tall trees make up the **canopy**. Bushes and small trees grow in the dark **understory**. Seeds, fallen leaves, and branches cover the forest floor. More than 100 inches (254 centimeters) of rain falls in the Amazon Rain Forest every year. The rain and high temperatures make the forest a steamy place.

9

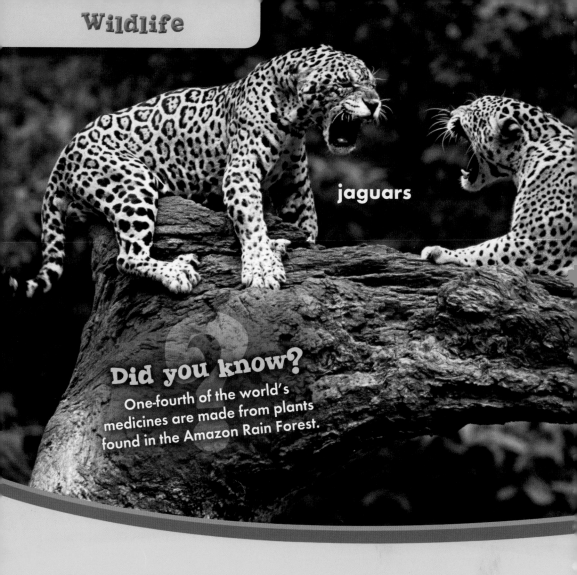

jaguars

Did you know?
One-fourth of the world's medicines are made from plants found in the Amazon Rain Forest.

The Amazon region has a greater variety of plants and animals than any other place in the world. Colorful parrots and toucans fly through the treetops. Monkeys swing from branch to branch. Slow-moving **sloths** hang from trees by their hooked claws. Jaguars and black panthers hunt on the forest floor. Anacondas, boa constrictors, and other snakes also hunt for prey. Insects like termites and leaf-cutter ants grind up leaves and dead trees to keep the soil healthy.

toucan

sloth

piranha

fun fact

Deadly piranhas swim in the rivers of the Amazon region. These small fish have sharp teeth and powerful jaws. Piranhas quickly tear the skin and flesh from their prey and leave just the bones behind.

The rest of Brazil is also rich with wildlife. Storks, herons, and other water birds build nests in the **wetlands**. This area is also home to **tapirs**, giant anteaters, and alligators called caimans. Sharks, dolphins, and whales share the waters off the coast with many other animals.

With about 201 million people, Brazil is the world's fifth most populated country. About half of all people in South America live in Brazil. Brazilians come from many backgrounds. Many have **ancestors** who came from Portugal, Spain, Germany, or other European countries. These early settlers journeyed to Brazil to farm and mine the land.

Some Brazilians have ancestors who were brought by force to Brazil from Africa. They worked as slaves on large farms. A small number of Brazilians have roots in Japan, China, Korea, and other Asian countries. Native peoples of Brazil also make up a small part of the population. Today, many Brazilians claim a mixed background.

Speak Portuguese!

Most Brazilians speak Portuguese because many of Brazil's original settlers were from Portugal. However, Brazilian Portuguese is not the same as the Portuguese spoken in Portugal.

English	Portuguese	How to say it
hello	oi	OY
good-bye	tchau	CHOW
yes	sim	SING
no	não	NAOWN
please	por favor	POHR fah-VOR
thank you	obrigado	oh-brih-GAH-doh
friend (male)	amigo	ah-MEE-goh
friend (female)	amiga	ah-MEE-gah

Where People Live in Brazil

countryside
14%

cities 86%

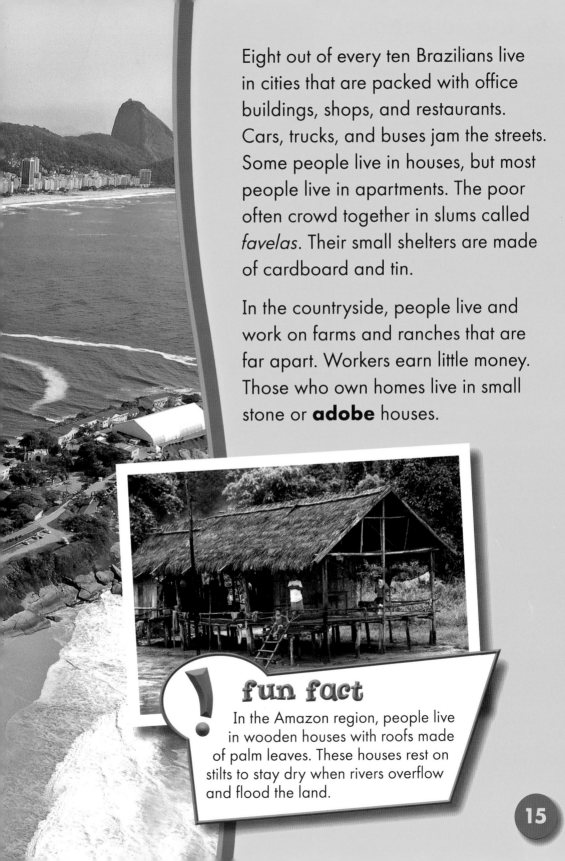

Eight out of every ten Brazilians live in cities that are packed with office buildings, shops, and restaurants. Cars, trucks, and buses jam the streets. Some people live in houses, but most people live in apartments. The poor often crowd together in slums called *favelas*. Their small shelters are made of cardboard and tin.

In the countryside, people live and work on farms and ranches that are far apart. Workers earn little money. Those who own homes live in small stone or **adobe** houses.

fun fact

In the Amazon region, people live in wooden houses with roofs made of palm leaves. These houses rest on stilts to stay dry when rivers overflow and flood the land.

Children in Brazil must go to school from ages 7 to 14. The schools are crowded. Most students are in class about four hours a day in either the morning or afternoon. They study reading, writing, math, and science. In some parts of Brazil, students must take a test to go on to the next grade. Students who go to high school can choose between two types of schools. One prepares them for university. The other offers training for jobs that they can start after graduating. Education is free in Brazil from kindergarten through university. Still, many students drop out to earn money for their families. Some students who leave school never learn to read and write.

Where People Work in Brazil

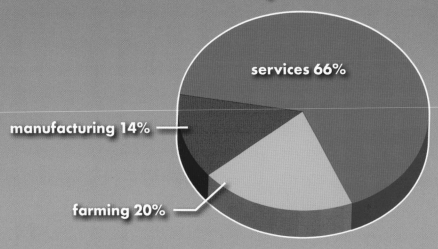

services 66%

manufacturing 14%

farming 20%

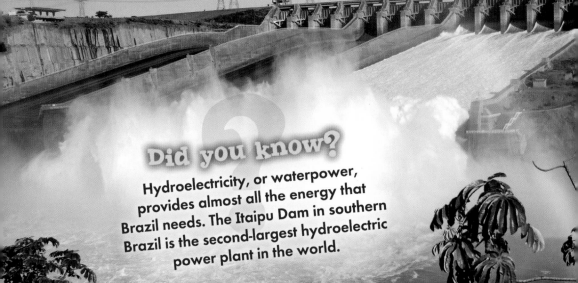

Did you know?

Hydroelectricity, or waterpower, provides almost all the energy that Brazil needs. The Itaipu Dam in southern Brazil is the second-largest hydroelectric power plant in the world.

Most Brazilian workers have **service jobs**.
They work in schools, government offices, hospitals,
and banks. Those who work in the restaurants, shops,
and large hotels that line Brazil's beaches serve millions
of visitors every year. Other Brazilians make cars,
airplanes, food products, and steel. They work in the
many factories around São Paulo.

Mining and farming are big businesses in Brazil's
countryside. Workers dig up **minerals** such as
iron ore, copper, tin, and gold. Brazilian ranchers
raise cattle, hogs, and chickens. Farmers grow
sugarcane, cotton, and much of the world's coffee.

Brazilians enjoy free time with family and friends. They gather in the evening to watch popular TV soap operas called *telenovelas*. Brazilian films draw people to movie theaters. People also go dancing to the beats of *bossa nova*, *samba*, and *lambada* music. Most Brazilians live within a few hours of the coast. They head to the white, sandy beaches to swim, surf, and sail.

The most popular sport in Brazil is soccer, or *futebol*. Nearly every city, town, neighborhood, and school has its own team. Brazilians also enjoy basketball, volleyball, and **motor sports**.

Brazilian soccer fans look forward to the World Cup, which is held every four years. More than 30 soccer teams from around the world compete in this event. Brazil is the only country that has played in every World Cup!

Did you know?
Brazilians eat everything with a fork in their left hand and a knife in their right hand. Touching food with your hands is considered bad manners in Brazil.

churrasco

feijoada

Meal preparation in Brazil often starts with a trip to the farmer's market, or *feira*. Shoppers find fruits, vegetables, grains, meat, and fish at these open-air markets. On Saturdays, families feast on *feijoada*. This mix of meat, black beans, and rice is Brazil's national dish. *Churrasco*, or grilled meat, and *almôndegas*, or meatballs, are other popular foods. Banana, coconut, and pepper flavors spice up many dishes. In the Amazon region, people cook up fresh fish pulled from rivers. Brazilians drink strong black coffee, or *cafezinho*. Fruit juices and a tea called *maté* are also popular drinks.

Carnaval

Most Brazilians are **Catholic**. They celebrate many religious holidays, including Christmas and Easter. The biggest holiday is *Carnaval*. This four-day party leads up to the Christian season of **Lent**. Thousands of people come to Rio de Janeiro for *Carnaval*. They wear colorful costumes and dance in the streets. Parades with huge floats draw cheers from the crowds. Brazilians also come together on September 7 for Independence Day. They celebrate the day in 1822 when Brazil became a country. There are parades and fireworks. People wave flags and streamers to show how proud they are to be Brazilian!

Christ the Redeemer

Christ the Redeemer is a famous statue in Brazil. This figure of Jesus Christ with his arms stretched wide stands on Mount Corcovado high above the city of Rio de Janeiro. Completed in 1931, Christ the Redeemer is one of the world's largest statues. It is about 100 feet (30 meters) tall. The statue sits on a large base that holds a chapel where visitors can gather. Christ the Redeemer is Brazil's most famous landmark. It is a symbol of peace that welcomes people to Brazil from around the world.

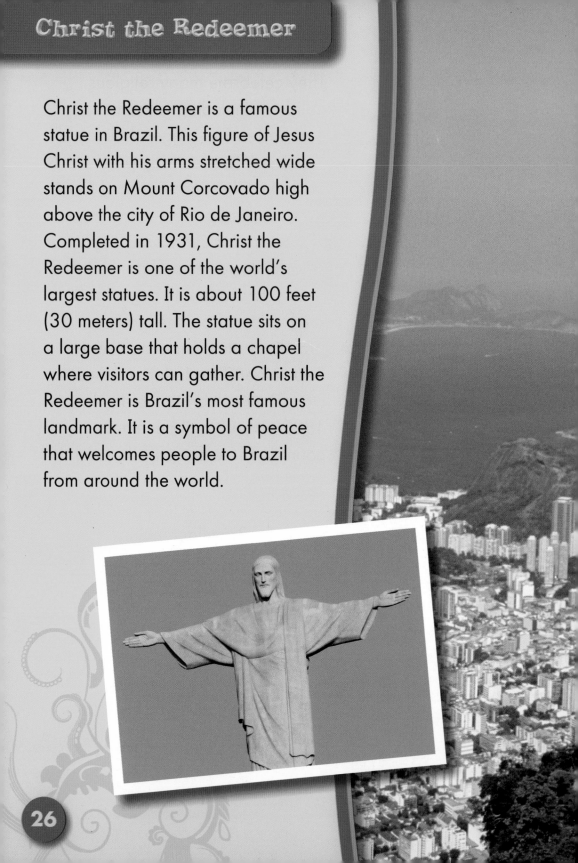

Did you know?

In 2007, people from around the world cast votes to choose the New Seven Wonders of the World. The Christ the Redeemer statue received many votes and was named a new wonder.

Fast Facts About Brazil

Brazil's Flag

The Brazilian flag is green with a yellow diamond in the middle that holds a blue globe with 27 white stars. There is one star for each of Brazil's 26 states and one for the Federal District of Brasília. The stars form the same pattern as the stars in Brazil's night sky. The white band across the middle of the globe features Brazil's motto, *Ordem e Progresso*, which means "Order and Progress."

Official Name: Federative Republic of Brazil

Area: 3,287,612 square miles
(8,514,877 square kilometers);
Brazil is the 5th largest country
in the world.

Capital City:	Brasília
Important Cities:	São Paulo, Rio de Janeiro, Salvador
Population:	201,103,330 (July 2010)
Official Language:	Portuguese
National Holiday:	Independence Day (September 7)
Religions:	Christian (89%), Other (11%)
Major Industries:	farming, manufacturing, mining, services
Natural Resources:	iron ore, wood, farmland, fish, oil, natural gas
Manufactured Products:	cars, airplanes, chemicals, cement, shoes, clothing
Farm Products:	coffee, soybeans, wheat, rice, corn, sugarcane, cocoa, citrus fruits, beef
Unit of Money:	real; the real is divided into 100 centavos.

Glossary

adobe—bricks made of clay and straw that are dried in the sun

ancestors—relatives who lived long ago

canopy—the layer of a rain forest made of a thick covering of leafy branches formed by the tops of trees

Catholic—a member of the Roman Catholic Church; Roman Catholics are Christian.

continent—one of the seven main land areas on Earth; the continents are Africa, Antarctica, Asia, Australia, Europe, North America, and South America.

Lent—the forty days before the Christian holiday of Easter when Catholics fast

minerals—elements found in nature; gold, iron, and oil are examples of minerals.

motor sports—sports that use vehicles with engines; auto racing is a popular motor sport in Brazil.

native—originally from a place

plateau—an area of flat, raised land

service jobs—jobs that perform tasks for people or businesses

sloths—mammals with gray-brown fur, large eyes, flat heads, and small ears; sloths have two or three toes with long claws on each foot and are known for moving very slowly.

tapirs—large mammals that look like pigs with long noses; tapirs live in forests in parts of South America and Asia.

tropical rain forest—a thick, green forest that lies in the hot and wet areas near the equator; it rains about 200 days each year in many tropical rain forests.

understory—the layer of a rain forest below the canopy; the understory is made up of small trees and bushes.

wetlands—wet, spongy land; bogs, marshes, and swamps are wetlands.

To Learn More

AT THE LIBRARY
Campos, Maria de Fatima. *Victoria Goes to Brazil.*
London, U.K.: Frances Lincoln Children's Books,
2009.

Goalec, François. *Frederico: A Child of Brazil.*
Detroit, Mich.: Blackbirch Press, 2005.

Roop, Peter and Connie. *A Visit to Brazil.* Chicago,
Ill.: Heinemann Library, 2008.

ON THE WEB
Learning more about Brazil
is as easy as 1, 2, 3.

1. Go to www.factsurfer.com.

2. Enter "Brazil" into the search box.

3. Click the "Surf" button and you will see a list of
   related Web sites.

With factsurfer.com, finding more information is just
a click away.

Index

activities, 20

Amazon Rain Forest, 6, 8-9

Amazon region, 10, 11, 15, 23

Amazon River, 8

Brasília, 4, 5

capital (see Brasília)

Carnaval, 25

Catholicism, 25

Christ, Jesus, 26

Christ the Redeemer, 26-27

daily life, 14-15

education, 16-17

food, 22-23

holidays, 24-25

housing, 15

Iguaçu Falls, 7

Independence Day, 25

landscape, 6-7, 8, 9

language, 13

location, 4-5

peoples, 8, 9, 12-13

Rio de Janeiro, 4, 5, 25, 26

São Paulo, 4, 5, 19

sports, 20-21

wildlife, 10-11

work, 18-19

The images in this book are reproduced through the courtesy of: Juan Martinez, front cover, pp. 8-9, 11 (top & bottom), 26 (small); Maisei Raman, front cover (flag), p. 28; Joao Epparino, pp. 4-5; Elder Vieira Salles, p. 6; Gary Yim, p. 7; Loren McIntyre/Photolibrary, p. 8 (small); Luiz C. Marigo/Photolibrary, pp. 10-11; worldswildlifewonders, p. 11 (middle); Nina B, p. 12; Mark Schwettmann, pp. 14-15; Joerg Boethling/Photolibrary, p. 15 (small); Guenter Fischer/Photolibrary, pp. 16-17; Achim Pohl/Photolibrary, p. 16 (small); Florian Kopp/Photolibrary, pp. 18, 19 (left); Peter Horree/Alamy, p. 19 (right); Vinivius Tupinamba, pp. 20, 29 (bill); sportgraphic, p. 21; Michael C. Gray, p. 22; Joao Virissimo, p. 23 (top); Celso Pupo, p. 23 (bottom); B. Martinez/Photolibrary, pp. 24-25; Angelo Cavalli/Photolibrary, pp. 26-27; Ekaterina Pokovsky, p. 29 (coin).